Thomas Hooker:
Puritan Minister and Founder of the Connecticut Colony

by Julia Kneeland

Illustrated by Rebekah Budd

Mecate Press

an imprint of Ricketts-White Design

Waterford

Dedicated to:

Elianna Jewell Kneeland
&
Aurora Rayne Kneeland

No part of this publication may be reproduced in whole or in part, or stored in a retrieval system, or transmitted in any form or by any means, electronic, mechanical, photocopying, recording, or otherwise without written permission of the publisher. For information regarding permission, write to Mecate Press, Ricketts-White Design 103 Butlertown Road, Waterford, CT 06385, www.mecatepress.com

Thomas Hooker, Puritan Minister and Founder of the Connecticut Colony was written by Julia Kneeland, www.juliakneeland.net

ISBN 978-0-9970342-8-8

Library of Congress Control Number: 2022916357

Illustrated by Rebekah Budd
Cover and book design by Judy Ricketts-White

Copyright © 2022 Julia Kneeland
Published by Mecate Press, Ricketts-White Design, Waterford, CT.
All rights reserved. Printed in the U.S.A.

Thomas Hooker played an important role in Connecticut's history. First, he fled his home in England and later came to America. He wanted to have freedom to worship as he believed. Next, he and his followers left Colonial Massachusetts. They sought freedom from the colony's strict leadership. Finally, he started the Connecticut Colony. He also helped create a new constitutional form of government for the very first time!

Thomas Hooker is known as the founder of Connecticut. What does it mean to be a founder of a new colony, and why is that important?

A founder is a person who is among the first to settle in a new area. Hooker and his followers wanted to leave their colony of Massachusetts. They thought that settling someplace new offered them a fresh start. They desired freedom from the rule of the church's stern leaders. Together they made their way to Connecticut.

It was significant that Thomas Hooker settled a new colony. Settling in Connecticut gave the colonists an opportunity to live where they had a say in how they were governed.

Thomas Hooker's life began in a peaceful quiet village in Marfield, England. The village was surrounded by open fields and \woods. This was a pastoral setting with thatched covered homes.

The church bells tolled, and Thomas and his family made their way to Saint Peter's Church in nearby Tilton. This magnificent stone structure sat high on a hill. The family attended church there on Sundays. Going to services was an essential part of their lives.

As Thomas progressed through school, he became greatly influenced by the Puritan beliefs. He attended colleges that wanted changes for the Church of England.

Soon after receiving his degree from Emmanuel College, he realized he should become a minister. He felt the desire to serve God and others, and that's exactly what he did his entire lifetime.

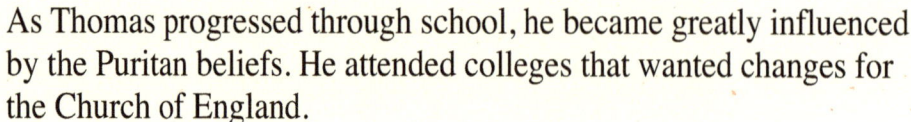

His career began as a minster at the Parish of Escher. While there he met and fell in love with Susanna Garband. They married on April 3, 1621.

Later, Hooker got a position as a preacher at Saint Mary's Church in Chelmsford, Essex. Unfortunately, he was kicked out because of his Puritan beliefs. Some of the nearby ministers had complained about him to the Church of England. This made Thomas upset especially because he believed he was doing the right thing.

Shortly after Thomas Hooker was called to appear in court because of his Puritan beliefs. He secretly boarded a ship and sailed for Holland. He fled England. He had to flee England or face harsh punishment.

Some Puritans were put in prison and had their property taken away.

Their churches were made to be plain and simple. They did not have fancy stained-glass windows. Also, they did not allow artwork and statues of saints. They even held services without instruments. This made singing hymns a challenge.

After leaving England, Hooker and his family travelled to this new colony, Massachusetts. He knew there he would be free to be a Puritan minister. They boarded the ship, "Griffin" with several other Puritan ministers.

On the long journey, the ministers preached. The people sang Psalms and prayed. They arrived in Boston eight weeks later.

Shortly after getting to Boston, Hooker became a minister in Newtown. There were about one hundred families in that town. Many of the people were considered wealthy. They owned land and cattle.

Hooker was a good Puritan minister. Because of this, he was asked to take part in Roger Williams' trial. Williams did not agree with other Massachusetts Puritan ministers. So, Hooker was asked to help him change his mind.

Hooker could not change Williams' mind. Williams was kicked out of the Massachusetts colony. Due to his beliefs, he felt that the church and state should be separate. Also, he thought taking land from the Native Americans was wrong. Roger Williams and his followers left Massachusetts. They settled the new colony of Rhode Island.

Following this trial, Hooker returned to Newtown. It became obvious to him that the members of the church were unhappy. They felt that the colony was governed too strictly by the church leaders. Hooker agreed with them.

The Newtown church asked the Massachusetts leaders for more land. They wanted to settle in a new place. At first, they were told no. Finally, they got permission to seek more land in a new area.

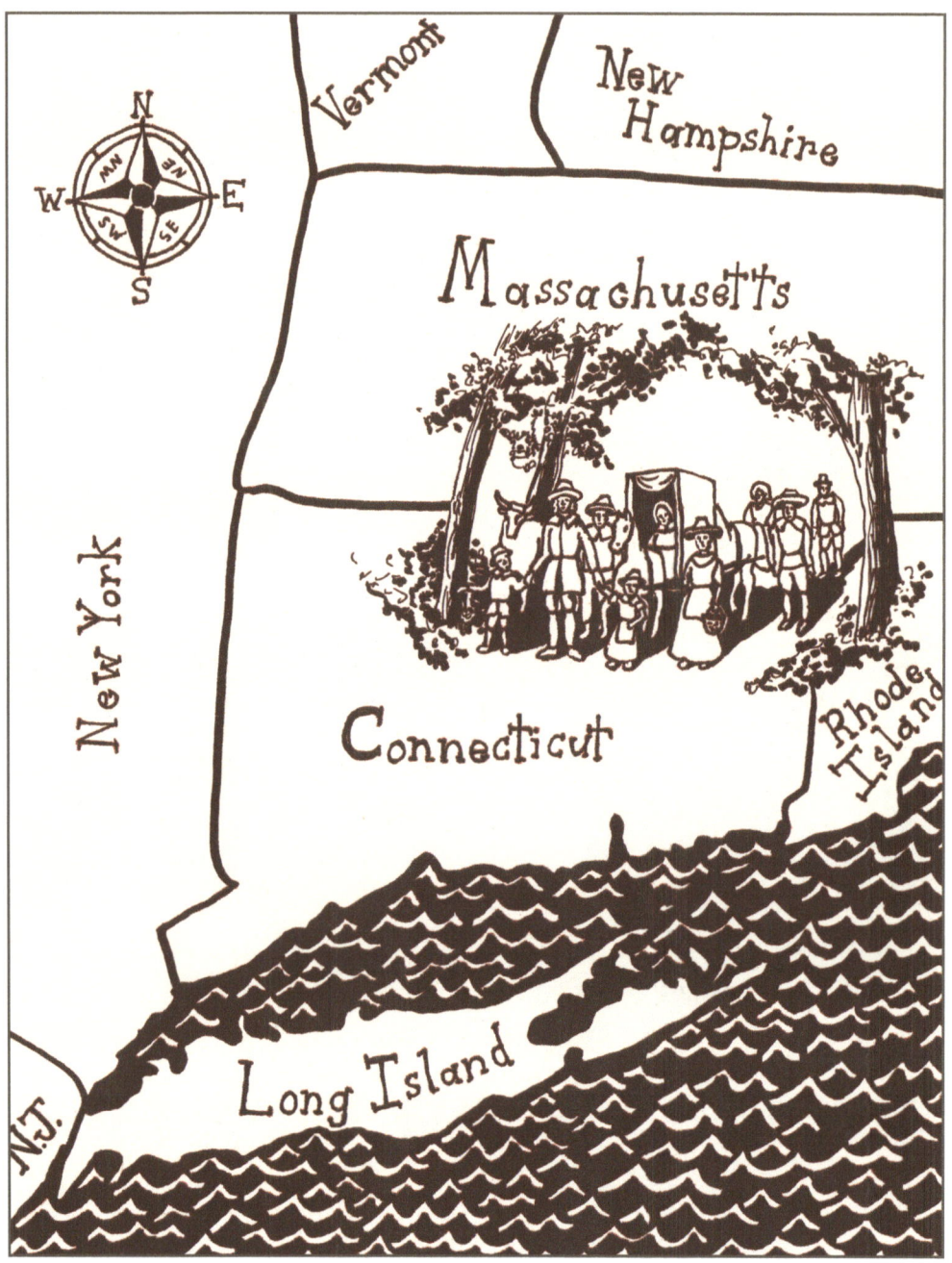

Hooker plus one hundred people started on their way. It was a long journey, but the colonists felt excited. They would now be free from the bonds of the Massachusetts colony.

The settlers walked along rugged Native American paths. The trip took two weeks. They brought their cattle, goats and pigs with them. Sometimes they would camp near a Native American village. They would share food together with the natives.

At one point they came to a large, wide river. The water was high that time of year because of the melted northern snows. The settlers were faced with a problem. How would they get themselves and their animals across the river? Thankfully, the Native Americans came to help them out.

One of the Native American leaders asked the nearby native villagers to bring canoes and rafts. These were used to carry the groups of settlers across the river. When they arrived on the other side of the river they continued south. This would later be where Hartford was settled.

Once they arrived in this new area, the colonists had a celebration. They were grateful for their safe journey. Also, they looked forward to a new beginning for themselves and their families.

As leader of this group, Thomas Hooker faced many challenges. He was busy setting up new homes and a church. He also set up regular church services. He felt his most important job was to minister to his people.

Hooker was a minister and a statesman. He was interested in how the colony would be governed. At first, the colony was governed by Massachusetts. Later, there was a meeting held in Hartford, and a new local government was started. One of the first things they decided was to form a group of colonists to fight the Native Americans.

Sadly, conflicts had arisen with the Native Americans. Many settlers had been killed by them, and two young girls were taken captive. Because of this the colonists decided to attack the Pequot Fort. This attack was quick and horrible. Several hundred Native Americans were killed within an hour's time. This was a victory for the colonists.

Later that year, Hooker was asked to take part in the trial of Anne Hutchinson. The trial took place in Boston. Anne was on trial because she did not believe the Puritan ministers were needed. She held meetings at her home that a group of colonists attended. She encouraged this group to not listen to their ministers.

At the end of her trial she was found guilty. She then was banished or kicked out of the Massachusetts Colony. Later, she and her followers settled in Rhode Island.

After her trial Hooker returned to Hartford. He spoke to the general court on how the colony should be governed. He believed all men had the right to vote. This was unlike the Massachusetts Colony. There they required church membership in order to vote.

Hooker addressed the general court. He gave ideas for the Fundamental Orders of Connecticut. These Orders explained how the government was set up by the people. They were in line with Puritan beliefs. Also, they allowed all men from the colony a right to vote. They did not need to be members of the church.

The Fundamental Orders were accepted by the colonists. This was considered the first constitution. A constitution sets up the rules for a state or country. These Orders became a model for other governing documents. This included the United States Constitution. The Fundamental Orders state that Connecticut was a separate colony from Massachusetts. Basically, they gave the right to govern to the people. These people did not seek approval from the church or king.

Thomas Hooker was an important colonial leader. He bravely settled a new colony. In addition, he helped to create a new colonial government. Hooker led his people with courage and wisdom. He never lost his desire to serve God and others. Thomas died July 7, 1647, from an epidemic that affected many colonists and Native Americans. Thomas Hooker will always be remembered as a respected man of God and seeker of religious freedom.

Thomas Hooker Timeline

July 7, 1586 —	Thomas Hooker was born in Marfield in Leicester County, England
Education —	Grammar School: Market Bosworth (West of Marfield 25 miles) Queens College, Cambridge
March 24, 1603 —	Death of Queen Elizabeth Accession of: James VI from Scotland to English Monarchy
1604 —	Emmanuel College, Cambridge (A distinctly Puritan institution)
January 1608 —	BA Degree: Emmanual College
1611 —	MA Degree: Emmanual College (Conversion after Master's Degree)
1618 —	Remained at Emmanual College
1618 — 1620 —	Thomas Hooker got Rectorship (Preached) at Parish of Esher in Surrey
1620 —	Plymouth Colony was founded by Pilgrims who desired to separate from Church of England
April 3, 1621 —	Married Susanna Garbrand (Mrs. Drake's waiting woman from Esher)
1626 —	Thomas Hooker became Lecturer at St. Mary at Chelmsford, Essex (As Lecturer preached on market days and Sunday afternoons)
1629 —	Thomas Hooker had to give up Lectureship and took a job as a schoolmaster in Little Baddow
1630 —	The Puritans came to America and settled the Massachusetts Bay Colony (They did not want to break away from the Church of England but wanted to purify it or reform it)

July 1630—	Thomas Hooker and his family left Old Park and secretly got aboard a vessel and sailed to Holland
1630—1633—	Thomas Hooker was first a resident of Amsterdam, later of Delft, and was two years in Rotterdam
July 10, 1633—	Thomas Hooker and family took the ship the "Griffin" and sailed to America (the journey took eight weeks)
September 4, 1633—	Arrived in Boston
October 11, 1633—	Thomas Hooker ordained as Pastor of Newtown, Massachusetts
October 9, 1635—	Thomas Hooker participated in the trial of Roger Williams (he was banished from Massachusetts Bay Colony)
June 1636—	Thomas Hooker and family plus one hundred people traveled to Connecticut
May 1, 1637—	Connecticut colonists declared war on the Native Americans—Pequots
November 7, 1637—	Thomas Hooker participated in the trial of Anne Hutchinson—she was found guilty and banished from the Massachusetts Bay Colony
May 31, 1638—	Thomas Hooker preached before the General Court of Connecticut: This sermon became the basis for The Connecticut Fundamental Orders
January 14, 1639—	The Fundamental Orders accepted as the basis of Government for the Colony of Connecticut
July 7, 1647—	Thomas Hooker died of "epidemical sickness"

Bibliography

Facts About Thomas Hooker–www.landofthebrave.info/thomas-hooker.htm

Thomas Hooker, 1586–1647, Father of American Democracy
    Chapter 6: The Dutch Disillusionment 1631–1633
    The English Reformer Becomes the American Founder

The Importance of Being Puritan: Church and State in Colonial Connecticut, By: Nancy Finlay
    https://connecticuthistory.org/the-importance-of-being-puritan-church-and-state-in-colonial-connecticut/

Journal Article – Thomas Hooker, The New England Quarterly Vol 25, No. 4 (December 1952) pp 459–488, by: Clinton Rossiter

Churches Were the Pillars Around Which State's Towns Were Built, By: Jesse Leavenworth, The Hartford Courant, August 3, 2014

Thomas Hooker: Connecticut's Founding Father/Connecticut History, By: Nancy Finlay, https://connecticuthistory.org/thomas-hooker-connecticuts-founding-father/

The Fundamental Orders of Connecticut/ConnecticutHistory.org
    https://connecticuthistory.org, inspired by Thomas Hooker's sermon of May 31, 1638

The Life of Roger Williams: the Founder of the State of Rhode Island by: William Gammell, 1812–1889, https://archive.org/details/lifeofrogerwilli00gamme

Society of the Descendants of the Founders of Hartford: Reverend Thomas Hooker
    The Founders of Hartford, http://www.foundersofhartford.org/founders/Hooker_thomas.htm

Thomas Hooker Facts, https://thehistoryjunkie.com/thomas-hooker-facts/

Thomas Hooker and the Democracy of Early Connecticut by: Perry Gilbert Miller
    The New England Quarterly, Vol. 4, No. 4 (Oct. 1931) pp. 663-712

Thomas Hooker by: Warren S. Archibald; Tercentenary Commission of State of Connecticut, January 1, 1933
Thomas Hooker, the First American Democrat; an address by: Walter Logan 1847–1906

The Connecticut Colony by: Johanna Johnston, Crowell-Collier Press, Collier-Macmillan Limited, London

About the Author

Julia Kneeland is a retired schoolteacher who loves to write! When she taught language arts, she used her own writing as samples for the students. They loved it! While growing up, she always enjoyed reading historical biographies. When she was teaching, she designed a language arts biography unit for her students. The focus was on people who influenced others. Thomas Hooker is an excellent example of this influence.

See more of her work at www.juliakneeland.net.

Rebekah Budd, Illustrator

Rebekah Budd was born and raised in Connecticut, on a farm adjacent to The Connecticut trail. She earned her Associates in Fine arts from Manchester Community College and received her Bachelors in Studio Fine Arts from SMFA at Tufts. One of her goals since childhood has been to be an illustrator, and this is the first book of her illustration career.

www.ingramcontent.com/pod-product-compliance
Lightning Source LLC
Chambersburg PA
CBHW041437010526
44118CB00002B/105